Gallivanting Granny

♥ Teaching you how to live vicariously
through the children in your life!

♥ Doing this without a computer

by

Linda Barlogio

Gallivanting With Me

Corona, California

Gallivanting Granny

Published by
Gallivanting with Me
Corona, California

Copyright © 2015 by *Linda Barlogio*

Second Edition

Illustrations by Linda Barlogio

Disclaimer: The Publisher and the Author does not guarantee that anyone following the techniques, suggestions, tips, ideas or strategies will become successful. The advice and strategies contained herein may not be suitable for every situation. The Publisher and Author shall have neither liability nor responsibility to anyone with respect to any loss or damage caused, or alleged to be caused, directly or indirectly by the information in this book. Any citations or a potential source of information from other organizations or websites given herein does not mean that the Author or Publisher endorses the information/content the website or organization provides or recommendations it may make. It is the readers' responsibility to do their own due diligence when researching information. Also, websites listed or referenced herein may have changed or disappeared from the time that this work was created and the time that it is read.

ISBN: 978-0-9905747-2-9 (paperback)

Printed in the United States of America

To all grandparents everywhere,
who want to spend more time with
their grandchildren. ❤

Dear Reader,

After hearing several grannies share their desire to have a closer relationship with their grandchildren, I wrote this book with them in mind, especially those that, for one reason or another, don't get to see the children in their lives often.

My sincere hope is that you will not only enjoy the wacky story, but that you will complete the activity in the back and invite your grandchild to play with you by sending them the thin Granny version of yourself, the passport, and the letter with simple instructions. (Don't worry – I included a sample!)

It's a great way for you to visit their day-to-day life and adventures and begin to interact with them in the activities and topics that are important to them.

I know that you will cultivate happy memories about the places you and your extraordinary kids have visited. It might even be fun to create an Adventure Album for all the pictures they send, especially if you do the activity with more than one grandchild.

Happy gallivanting!

Linda Barlogio

Once upon a time, long ago, in a faraway land called Los Angeles, lived Granny and her dog, Dusty. She lived in a mobile home park and had a wonderful neighbor, Molly. But sometimes, Granny felt very lonely because her grandchildren lived far away in places like St. Louis, Missouri; Chico, California; New Ulm, Minnesota; and Knoxville, Tennessee. There are even more places, but it's hard to remember all of them!

Granny wished with all her heart that she could visit these children, but she had bunions and rheumatism (ouch!), so it was difficult to get around. Besides, she hated to fly. She thought it was scary!

One day, she and Molly talked about their grandchildren and how little they got to see them. When Granny told her friend about her dreams to visit the children, Molly encouraged Granny to do more than just dream: "Maybe go on a plane OR get on Facebook?" Granny shook her head. Granny thought Facebook was scary too, and she hated computers!

What can I do? she asked herself. Suddenly, it came to her!

The most practical thing for me to do is wish on the first

star in the evening sky. Then, when I go to sleep, maybe I will

dream up some ideas about how I can visit my grandchildren.

She closed her eyes and drifted off.

The next morning, Granny didn't have an answer, but one was about to hit her – literally!

She was out walking on the grass near her mobile home and didn't hear the riding lawn mower coming. Her hearing is sometimes bad and besides, her mind was on other things... like her wish. Jim, the gardener, doesn't always see too well either and Granny was wearing a green dress and green shoes that blended right in with the grass!

Oh......give me a home.... where the Buffalo Roam!

Suddenly, one of the big tires ran smack over her! Jim felt the bump, but when Granny jumped up and seemed okay, he just kept mowing and singing his favorite song! Granny rushed home and was so flummoxed by the whole incident that she fell into bed and went straight to sleep.

When Granny woke up, she was paper-thin! *I always wanted to be thin, but this is preposterous,* she thought as she looked at her reflection.

As usual, Molly came over for a cup of tea and scones. When she saw Granny, she exclaimed, "Oh, my gosh!"

How could this be? Granny seemed okay. She was talking and walking, BUT she was unbelievably thin, so thin you could almost see through her! She was as thin as a piece of paper, thin as a ribbon, thin as a rail, thin as a... oh, you get the picture!

Molly was absolutely flabbergasted! She thought they should call someone – maybe the fire department or a doctor. How could they explain this? Would anyone believe them?

At that moment, the doorbell rang and in walked Marilyn, another neighbor. She, too, couldn't believe her eyes! There was Granny, practically transparent! Molly was glad that Marilyn was there so they could sit and talk about what to do.

It was hard for Granny to sit down because her knees were stiff and didn't bend properly, but she did sit down so she could discuss this predicament with her friends.

Right out of the blue, Marilyn laughed and said, "Why don't we mail Granny to one of her grandchildren? Since she is as thin as a piece of paper, it would work! Maybe she would even have an adventure or two and we could call her 'Gallivanting Granny!'"

Granny was very afraid of this idea. It would be dark and scary in the post office mailbox. It would be crowded with all the other mail, and it would hurt getting tossed around. You get the picture here, right? Granny always had lots of excuses to keep from going on adventures!

However, Molly and Marilyn finally talked her into it, and the next thing they did was go to the post office to get a VERY LARGE envelope.

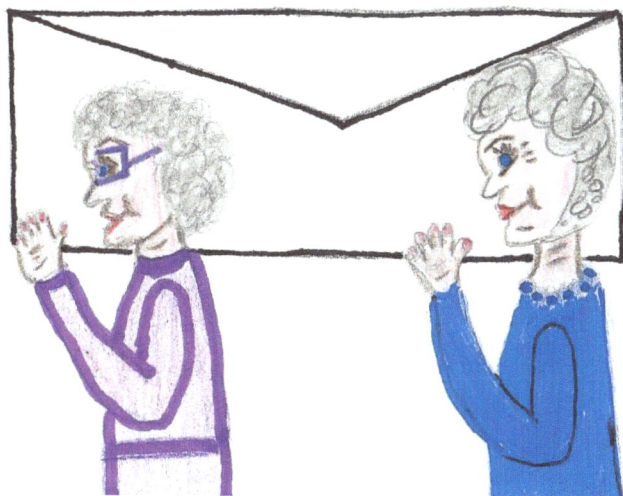

On the way back from the post office, they passed Marj's house. She was outside hanging up one of her amazing quilts to air it out. They explained Granny's predicament and asked for ideas. She suggested that they wrap Granny in a small quilt and mail her in one of the post office's snazzy boxes. Maybe it would give Granny a safer and more comfortable ride.

Marilyn and Molly thanked Marj for her suggestion, but thought that they should go with the original scheme and keep the quilt idea for the next Granny mailing.

When they got home, they wrote a letter to the family of each of Granny's grandchildren asking them to take 'Gallivanting Granny' on an adventure, "Take pictures with Granny and include information on the enclosed passport."

Last, but not least, they asked the families to put Granny, the Passport, and the pictures into another big envelope and return them to Granny's home.

In the end, even Gallivanting Granny got excited about her upcoming explorations. She knew that there was so much to see that she hadn't seen before. Gallivanting Granny could hardly wait to go on her first adventure!

Activity

1. **Make your thin Granny look like you!**

   Make her look as much like you as possible: hair color, eye color, glasses, etc. Her clothes can be your favorite: dresses, pants, or even a sweatshirt and blue jeans! You could possibly send along a coat for cold days or a sundress for sunny days. (Magazines can give ideas for dressing your "Granny".) Use all of the resources you have (crayons, markers, colored pencils, scrapbook paper, etc.) and remember that the children in your life are your audience - *not* the art critic for the local paper!

2. **Write a letter to your grandchild and invite them to play!**

   Not sure what to say? Don't fret! I've written up a sample letter on the next page, which includes the instructions. All you need to do is customize some of the words and phrases to make it sound like YOU wrote it!

3. **Get your passport ready.**

   Cut out the passport pages and then staple, glue, or ribbon-tie them together.

4. **Send your Granny, your letter, and the passport to your grandchild!**

5. **Let the FUN begin!**

Sample Letter

Customize it with your own words and phrases.

Dear _____,

    I am sending this letter because I would love to go on adventures with you. You are probably wondering how I can do that since I live in _____ and you are in _____. But, I have recently become acquainted with someone who can help us.

    Her name is Gallivanting Granny! Can you see the resemblance? She's a super thin version of me! I had to make her thin, so I could send her through the mail.

    I would love it if you would please let her (Me!) accompany you on some of your favorite day-to-day activities such as visits to the store, the park, or on any fantastic adventures you might have. I really want to see for myself where you go and what you do!

    How will I see? Good question!

    Well, you'll have to ask your _____ to take a picture of you and Granny wherever you go. When you have taken your pictures, ask your _____ to print them out so you can put them in this handy-dandy passport I've sent you and then tell me (on the page next to the picture) where you were when you took the picture and what you liked about your adventure there.

    I hope this will be fun for you. I can't wait to see the pictures, with me included, and hear about all of your exciting escapades!

All my love,

GALLIVANTING GRANNY'S PASSPORT

Granny visited here: _____

With: _____

On: _____

Granny visited here: —————

With: ——————

On: ——————

Granny visited here: —————

With: ——————

On: ——————

Granny visited here: _____

With: _____

On: _____

Granny visited here: _____

With: _____

On: _____

Granny visited here: _____

With: _____

On: _____

Granny visited here: _____

With: _____

On: _____

Granny visited here: _____

With: _____

On: _____

Granny visited here: _____

With: _____

On: _____

Granny visited here: _____

With: _____

On: _____

THE END

Continue the Adventure

Please send pictures and stories about the escapades "you" and your kids
have taken if you would like to share them with other grannies.
Linda anticipates putting together a book of these wonderful adventures,
so we can inspire others to go on their own adventures!

Contact Linda if you would like to surprise your granny friends with
a fun workshop experience where they can have an enjoyable time
and learn some easy techniques to improve communication
with their grandchildren as well as to manage the change that happens
when these wonderful children come into our lives!

An easy way to stay connected with Linda is to visit:
www.GallivantingWithMe.com

**Stay tuned for new adventures with Granny.
More books to come!**

About the Author

After working as an adjunct counselor and instructor for more than 14 years, Linda Barlogio recently retired from Chaffey Community College where it was her passion to help students figure out what they wanted to do when they grew up – something she says she is still working on for herself!

As a mother, grandmother, educator, and counselor, Linda has experienced the reality that communication across the generations is not easy. We all have expectations that are not readily met, and this is where the stressful situations arise. She received her Master's in Education, with a focus on counseling from the University of Redlands and then worked for 18 years with both young and mature adults in the field of Education and realized that communication issues are at the heart of all counseling dilemmas. When she discussed these dilemmas with her friend, Marilyn, who is a psychologist, they realized just how important it was to fill this communication gap with grandparents. Thus the idea for this book was born. Linda knew she had to write it and get it to as many grannies as she could!

By writing *Gallivanting Granny* and conducting corresponding workshops with grannies in her community, Linda's mission is to give support to grandparents in their attempts to play a bigger part in their children's lives.

Linda lives in Corona, California with her husband, Jim, and their dog, Dusty. She has three children, seven grandchildren, and numerous nieces and nephews.

❤️ **Thank you to...** ❤️

Marilyn Rock, for your knowledge, thoughtful inspiration, and friendship.

Marj Grayck, for your courage, support, and love.

Molly Dillon, for your wonderful writing expertise and friendship.

Wendy Whitney, for your delightful first critique that didn't include, "You've lost your mind!"

Cynthia Ulloa, for your push to get me doing my own illustrations.

Vernette Mackley, for your very long-time friendship and kind, generous support.

Aurora Lavado, for your clarity and insight just when I needed it most!

All the students at Chaffey College and Corona-Norco Adult Education, for the challenges and struggles that you have overcome. You have helped me find my own courage to take a risk too and get out of my comfort zone.

My husband, Jim, for your quiet patience with the outlandish schemes I often pursue.

And last, but not least, Amanda Johnson and True to Intention. Without you all, this book would still be a "good intention" and we all know what happens with those!

www.ingramcontent.com/pod-product-compliance
Lightning Source LLC
Chambersburg PA
CBHW060854270326
41934CB00002B/140